Reconciliation

The Subcommittee on the Catechism, United States Conference of Catholic Bishops, has found this text, copyright 2011, to be in conformity with the *Catechism of the Catholic Church*; it may be used only as supplemental to other basal catechetical texts.

Nihil Obstat: Rev. William M. Becker, STD

        Censor Librorum

        April 5, 2011

Imprimatur: †Most Rev. John M. Quinn, DD

        Bishop of Winona

        April 5, 2011

The nihil obstat and imprimatur are official declarations that a book or pamphlet is free of doctrinal or moral error. No implication is contained therein that those who have granted the nihil obstat or imprimatur agree with the contents, opinions, or statements expressed, nor do they assume any legal responsibility associated with publication.

The publishing team included Gloria Shahin, editorial director; Joanna Dailey, development editor and contributing writer, "Heart to Heart" feature; Maura Thompson Hagarty, PhD, theological reviewer; prepress and manufacturing coordinated by the production departments of Saint Mary's Press.

Scripture story and cover illustrations created by Vicki Shuck.

Printed in the United States of America

2324 (PO6996)

ISBN 978-1-59982-069-9

Reconciliation

Celebrate and Remember

Regina Anne Kelly

saint mary's press

All About Me

as I Prepare for My First Reconciliation

A Picture of Me

A Picture of
My Family

A Picture of My
Parish Church

My Name

_____

My Age

_____

My Family

_____

_____

_____

_____

My Parish

_____

A Picture that
Reminds Me of
My Faith

**My Favorite Thing about
My Catholic Faith**

_____

_____

_____

A Picture of Me
Celebrating My Faith
at Baptism or at Mass

**My First Reconciliation
Promises**

_____

_____

_____

_____

_____

A Picture of Jesus

**My Prayer to Jesus
to Help Me Prepare for
First Reconciliation**

_____

_____

_____

_____

_____

Contents

Open my eyes to see clearly

the wonders of your teachings.

Psalm 119:18

In the Name of the Father, and of the Son, and of the Holy Spirit

 The Sign of the Cross

In the name of the Father,

and of the Son,

and of the Holy Spirit.

Amen.

What Is Reconciliation?

God Forgives Us

The Bible tells a story about the first sin. This story helps to explain why people need God's forgiveness. In the Bible we read:

When God created the first man and first woman, he also created a wonderful garden for them.

Then God said to the man and the woman, "You may eat the fruit on all the trees that grow here. But do not eat the fruit of the tree of knowledge of good and evil."

The man and woman obeyed God. But then one day, there was a serpent in the garden. This serpent was sly and wicked. The serpent asked the man and woman why they did not eat from the tree of knowledge.

"We can eat all the fruits of all the trees except that one," answered the woman.

"Well," said the serpent, "God only said that because he does not want you to become as powerful and wise as he, knowing what is good and what is evil." This was a terrible lie.

The man and the woman believed the serpent's lie. So they took a piece of fruit and ate it.

Suddenly, they were no longer happy. They felt shame. They knew they had done wrong.

God still loved the people he had made, but they could no longer live in the beautiful garden. God had to send them away.

Based on Genesis 2:7–9,15–17; 3:1–24

Activity

When one person does something hurtful to another person, the two people need to come together and make peace. **Draw** a picture that shows two people making peace.

 **With My Family**

Visit the Web site of the United States Conference of Catholic Bishops (USCCB) to read about the first sin of human beings. Click on the Bible tab at the top of the page. Then click on Genesis, then Chapter 3. Read and talk about the Scripture passage.

Jesus Gives Us the Sacraments

A **sin** is something we say, do, or think that does not follow God's will. Sometimes we sin by not doing something we should. When we sin, we disobey God. We turn away from him and fail to act with love for him and for other people as Jesus did. We offend God and hurt our relationship with him and with other people.

The first sin of humankind is called **Original Sin.** This sin has been passed on to all of us. We are born with it. Original Sin weakens us and makes it harder for us to do what is right.

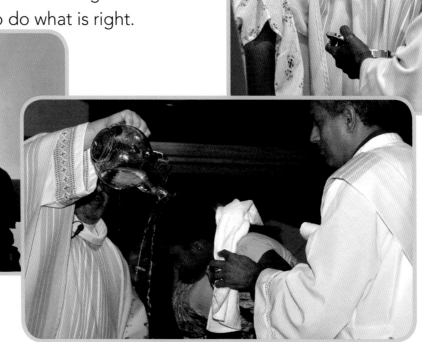

Three images on this page © Bill Wittman/www.wpwittman.com

We don't know why God allows sin in the world, but we are certain that he always loves us. He loved us so much that he sent his Son, Jesus Christ, into the world. Jesus died on the cross and rose again to free us from sin. When we are sorry for our sins, Jesus brings us back to God our Father. God forgives our sins. When God forgives us, we are reconciled with God and others. We are brought back together with God. One day, when we meet God face-to-face in Heaven, we'll understand his loving plan for the world and why allowing sin was part of it.

Jesus is the greatest sign of God's love. But Jesus gave seven more great and holy signs to God's people, the Church. These signs are called **Sacraments.** The Sacraments join us to Jesus so that we can follow him more closely. They give us **grace,** the free gift of God's own life in us. Grace makes us his children and helps us to stay away from sin and to do good works.

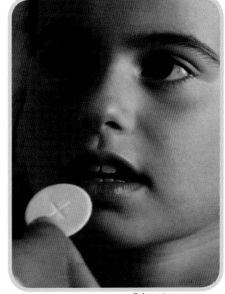

© AgnusImages.com

When we are reconciled with God and others, we are peaceful and happy. **Draw** yourself and your family being peaceful and happy together.

The Sacrament of Reconciliation

© The Crosiers/Gene Plaisted, OSC

We celebrate the Sacraments, especially the Eucharist, all through our lives. The three Sacraments that begin our life in the Church are the Sacraments of Baptism, Confirmation, and the Eucharist. We call these the Sacraments of Christian Initiation.

In the Sacrament of Baptism, we were baptized with holy water. Baptism united us to Jesus and gave us the Holy Spirit. We became members of God's people, the Church. The Church is the Body of Christ. All the members are united to Christ and to one another. Think of your own body and all of its parts. Think about your head, your eyes, your mouth, your hands, your feet, and your heart. The parts do many different things, but they are all important. And if they weren't part of a whole body, they would have no life. This helps us understand what it means to be a member of the Church, a member of Christ's body. Every member is united with Christ and all the other members. Each is different, but each is important. Every person has gifts that can help others follow Jesus.

In Baptism, all sins, including Original Sin, are washed away. Sins that we commit after Baptism are forgiven through the **Sacrament of Reconciliation.** If we choose to sin, we not only hurt our relationship with God. We also hurt our relationship with all of God's people, the Church. Jesus gave us the Sacrament of Penance and Reconciliation to bring us back to God when we sin. When we receive the Sacrament of Reconciliation, grace, God's own life in us, brings us back together with God and with one another.

Celebrating the Sacrament

The Sacrament of Reconciliation begins with the priest greeting us and welcoming us. Then we pray together, "In the name of the Father, and of the Son, and of the Holy Spirit," as we make the Sign of the Cross. The Sign of the Cross reminds us of our Baptism. It reminds us of God's life in us. It reminds us that Jesus died and rose for us. It reminds us that we belong to God.

Making the Sign of the Cross also reminds us about who God is. He is one God in three Persons: the Father, the Son, and the Holy Spirit. This mystery is called the Trinity. It is at the center of our faith.

© Bill Wittman/www.wpwittman.com

Activity

Write one word that describes a feeling that the Sacrament of Reconciliation can give you. **Decorate** the space around your word.

Living Our Faith

The Sacraments give us God's own life. If we come to them with faith in Jesus, God's grace will work in our lives.

With My Family

As a family, look at pictures or other mementos of your Baptism. Together say a prayer thanking God for his new life in you.

Heart to Heart

Forgiveness

Sometimes people hurt our feelings. Did any of your classmates ever play a game and not let you play? Think about the way you felt. It is especially hard when someone we love and care about hurts our feelings. Yet, sometimes we are the ones who hurt someone else's feelings. And then, when we think about what we did, we feel terrible.

When this happens, we need reconciliation. We need to forgive and we need to be forgiven. For this to happen, someone needs to say, "I'm sorry," and someone else needs to say, "I forgive you."

Two images on this spread © Rhienna Cutler/istockphoto.com

Activity

In the "Before Reconciliation" space on top, **draw** two people who are angry with each other or hurting each other. In the "After Reconciliation" space on the bottom, **draw** the same two people after they forgive each other and are reconciled.

Before Reconciliation

RECONCILIATION

After Reconciliation

Saint Spotlight

**Saint Teresa of Ávila
(1515–1562)**

Saint Teresa of Ávila is a saint from Spain. She wrote many books about prayer. She also wrote about sin. Saint Teresa wrote that when she sinned, she would ask God to forgive her. She would then make great efforts to become better.

With My Family

Together review the names of the Sacraments of Christian Initiation and the Sacrament of Reconciliation shown on pages 6 and 7. Share a personal experience related to each one.

We Pray Together

We Praise the Trinity

Leader: God, our Father, you created us out of love. You never stop loving us even when we sin.

All: Glory be to God the Father.

Leader: You sent your Son, Jesus, to teach us how to live and to show us how to forgive.

All: Glory be to God the Son.

Leader: You send your Holy Spirit to be our helper and guide and to give us the grace we need to turn away from sin.

All: Glory be to God the Holy Spirit.

Leader: For these wonderful gifts, we pray,

All: Glory be to the Father and to the Son and to the Holy Spirit, as it was in the beginning, is now, and ever shall be, world without end. Amen.

© Andrew Penner/istockphoto.com

10

Trust in God's Mercy

We Pray for God's Mercy

Leader: Let us pray for God's mercy.

Side 1: Have mercy on us, O God.

Side 2: For you are great and good.

Side 1: Wash away our sins.

Side 2: Heal our hearts.

Side 1: Open our lips.

Side 2: And we will praise you.

Side 1: Create clean hearts for us, O God.

Side 2: Give us joyful and willing spirits.

Side 1: We will tell others about you

Side 2: That they may know your goodness.

All: Lord, we praise and thank you with all our hearts!

Based on Psalm 51

Who Loves and Forgives Us?

The Forgiving Father

To teach us that God is our forgiving Father who rejoices when we are sorry for our sins, Jesus told this story.

A man had two sons. Each son would inherit money from the father one day, but the younger son did not want to wait. He asked his father for his share of the money. The father agreed.

A few days later, the younger son took all his money and left. He went away and spent everything he had on wasteful and selfish things.

Soon he was hungry and penniless. He did not know what to do, so he took a job feeding and caring for a farmer's pigs. He was so hungry, he almost ate the pig feed!

He thought, "My own father's servants are better fed than I am. I will go back to my father and say I am sorry. I no longer deserve to be called his son, but maybe he will take me back as a servant."

So he headed home. As he drew closer to home, his father saw him in the distance and ran to meet him. The father hugged and kissed his long-lost son.

The son said, "Father, I have sinned against heaven and against you. I no longer deserve to be called your son."

But the father was not angry. He was filled with love for his son and rejoiced at his return. The father held a great celebration to welcome his son home.

Based on Luke 15:11–24

Activity

The list below are words from the Scriptures. **Write** the correct word from the list to complete the word puzzle for *Forgive*.

rejoice **sin** **son** **sorry** **Father** **God** **love**

F ___ ___ ___ ___ ___

___ O ___

___ ___ R ___

___ G ___ ___

___ I ___

___ ___ V ___

___ E ___ ___ ___ ___ ___

With My Family

As a family, read together Luke 15:1–10. In these Scripture verses that come just before the story of the forgiving father, Jesus uses two other stories to illustrate God's forgiveness. What are these stories? Discuss the connection among all these stories.

God Sent Jesus to Forgive Sins

© Danny Lehman/Corbis

God knew that human beings needed his love and forgiveness. So God sent his Son, Jesus Christ, to bring us back to him and to save us from sin. The name "Jesus" means "God saves."

In the Scriptures, we find many stories about Jesus forgiving sinners. Jesus shared God's **mercy,** or love and forgiveness, with them. Jesus told the story of the forgiving father to teach us how much God the Father loves us. He wanted us to know that God always welcomes back sinners who are sorry for what they have done.

In the story of the forgiving father, the younger son knew he had done wrong. He admitted that he had sinned. When he went back to his father, he showed his sorrow and his contrition. **Contrition** means being sorry for our sins and trying not to sin again.

There are times when we are sorry, or have contrition, because of our love for God and our love for others. There are also times when we might be sorry because we will be scolded or punished for what we did. It is better to be sorry because of love for God and others than because of fear. But being sorry always means trying not to sin again.

© Tamara Bauer/istockphoto.com

Activity

When we are sorry for something we did, we have contrition. **Draw** yourself at a time when you were sorry for something you did.

The Church Forgives Sins in Jesus' Name

Jesus suffered, died on the cross, and rose again to bring us new life, now and forever. We first received this new life in Jesus Christ when we were baptized. In Baptism, God forgave our sins and gave us a promise of everlasting happiness with him. This is the happiness that God wanted us to have from the beginning of Creation. This is the perfect joy and happiness that awaits us in Heaven.

If we commit sins after receiving the Sacrament of Baptism, the Sacrament of Reconciliation gives us God's life again. In this Sacrament, our sins are forgiven through the words and actions of the priest or bishop. Just like the long-lost son, we come back to our Father. We can celebrate the gift of new life in Jesus, now and forever!

Two images on this page © Bill Wittman/www.wpwittman.com

Celebrating the Sacrament

When we celebrate the Sacrament of Reconciliation, the priest encourages us to remember that God is our forgiving Father. He invites us to trust in God's mercy:

Priest: "May God, who has enlightened every heart, help you to know your sins and trust in his mercy."

Response: "Amen."

(Rite of Penance)

Activity

Color all of the letters marked with a "+" to reveal a special message.

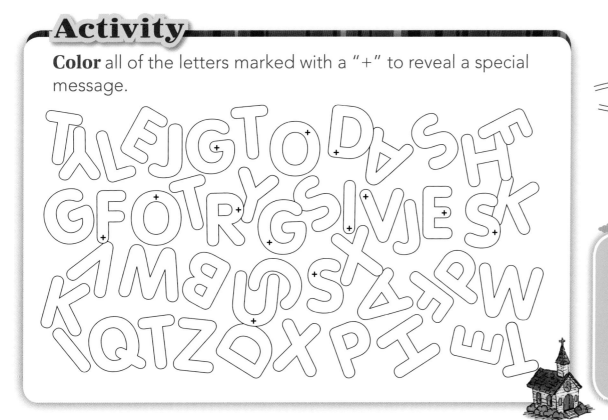

Faith Highlights

Only priests can forgive our sins in the Sacrament of Reconciliation.

With My Family

Together point to one or two important Catholic teachings about forgiveness that you have learned from these two pages.

Heart to Heart

God's Gift of New Life

Think about what it feels like to get a beautiful gift. You open it carefully or maybe you tear it open. Often you discover that it is just what you wanted! How would you care for that gift? Would you kick it around or leave it out in the rain? Or would you take good care of the gift so it will stay looking like new?

At your Baptism, the gift you received was God's life. When Original Sin was taken away, you were filled with the gift of grace. But now that you are older, sometimes doing what God wants is not so easy. Your parents and teachers can help you, but you are the only one who can decide to make good choices. And what happens when you don't? God's mercy is waiting for you, just like the forgiving father waited for his son and rejoiced at his return. In the Sacrament of Reconciliation, God's gift of life will make you new again!

Activity

In this lesson, you read the story of the forgiving father. In the maze below, **help** the lost son find his way back to the forgiving father.

Saint Spotlight

Saint Thérèse of the Child Jesus (1873–1897)

When Thérèse was a little girl, she found that she could follow Jesus by doing little things with great love. Thérèse was not perfect, but she always asked forgiveness of her parents and sisters when she did something wrong. This was part of her "little way" to God. Saint Thérèse taught us that asking forgiveness is something that everyone can do.

With My Family

Do research online and select a saint to be the "patron saint of forgiveness" for your family. Post a picture and a short paragraph about this saint on the refrigerator or a bulletin board at home.

We Pray Together

 ## We Pray for Forgiveness

Forgiving Father,

Your love for us is everlasting.

You are always ready to forgive.

Help us have forgiving hearts for those who have
hurt us in any way.

Help us make up with those whom we have hurt.

We ask this through your Son, Jesus Christ.

Amen.

© VeryBigAlex/shutterstock.com

20

We Follow God's Word

We Pray with the Word of God

Leader: Your Word, O Lord, is a light for our lives.

All: Your Word, O Lord, is a light for our lives.

Reader 1: Love the Lord, your God, with all your heart,

Reader 2: with all your soul, with all your mind, and with all your strength.

All: Your Word, O Lord, is a light for our lives.

Reader 3: Happy are they who obey God's rules

Reader 4: and seek the Lord with all their hearts.

All: Your Word, O Lord, is a light for our lives.

Reader 5: Be kind to one another

Reader 6: and forgive one another as God has forgiven you.

All: Your Word, O Lord, is a light for our lives.

Reader 7: If you keep my commandments, you will stay in my love.

Reader 8: Love one another as I have loved you.

All: Your Word, O Lord, is a light for our lives.

Based on Psalm 119:105; Deuteronomy 6:5; Psalm 119:2; Ephesians 4:32; John 15:10,12

What Are God's Rules?

God Tells Us How to Live

God first gave us rules for living a good life when he gave the Ten Commandments to Moses on Mount Sinai. God told Moses to share these Commandments with the Israelites to help them be faithful to him:

1. I am the Lord your God, you shall not have other gods before me.
2. You shall not take the name of the Lord your God in vain.
3. Remember to keep holy the Lord's Day.
4. Honor your father and your mother.
5. You shall not kill.
6. You shall not commit adultery.
7. You shall not steal.
8. You shall not bear false witness against your neighbor.
9. You shall not covet your neighbor's wife.
10. You shall not covet your neighbor's possessions.

Based on Exodus 19:20, 20:1–17

God fully revealed his rules for life through his Son, Jesus Christ. When Jesus was asked, "Which of the commandments is the greatest?" he answered:

"First, you shall love the Lord your God with all your heart, with all your soul, with all your mind, and with all your strength. Second, you shall love your neighbor as yourself." Jesus also said, "I give you a new commandment: Love one another as I have loved you."

Based on Mark 12:28–31, John 13:34

Reread the words that Jesus said in the Scriptures. What is the most important thing Jesus wants us to do? **Find** the word below and circle it. **Draw** a symbol for this word.

KNOW

LOVE

WORK

KEEP

HONOR

With My Family

As a family, talk about ways you can follow God's rules for life and love one another. Make a list together. Use the Ten Commandments and Jesus' teachings as the basis for your list.

The Ten Commandments are listed on page 85 in the back of this book.

The Scriptures Guide Us

The Bible, or Sacred Scripture, is the Word of God. God guided the writers of the Scriptures to write the teachings that he wanted us to know and follow.

The Word of God is a guide for our lives. It teaches us ways to be faithful to God. From the Scriptures we learn the Ten Commandments, God's rules for living in a faithful, loving relationship with him.

When Jesus came, he showed people how to follow God's rules perfectly. He taught that the meaning of the Ten Commandments is to love God and to love one another. We find Jesus' teachings in the Scriptures, especially in the four Gospels.

God Gave Us Rules Out of Love

God gave us rules out of love. To help us follow God's rules, Jesus gave us the Great Commandment: "You shall love the Lord your God with all your heart, with all your soul, with all your mind, and with all your strength; and you shall love your neighbor as yourself."

(Based on Mark 12:30–31)

Sin leads us away from God. We cannot sin by mistake or by accident. We sin when we make a deliberate choice to say, do, or want something that does not follow God's will.

© R. Gino Santa Maria /istockphoto.com

Activity

A sin is something we choose to do. A mistake or accident is something we do not choose to do. **Draw** yourself making a mistake or doing something by accident.

We Are Called to Follow Jesus

There are two kinds of sin. One kind is very serious. We call this **mortal sin.** Mortal sins are so serious that they completely break our loving relationship with God. We must seek God's forgiveness for mortal sins in the Sacrament of Penance and Reconciliation. We must confess a mortal sin before we can receive Holy Communion. A person who commits a mortal sin but does not confess it will be separated from God forever.

The second kind of sin is less serious. We call this kind of sin **venial sin.** Venial sins weaken, but do not completely break, our loving relationship with God. Venial sins hurt us, but they don't stop love for God and others from living in our hearts. Love can repair the damage venial sins cause.

© Charles Silvey/istockphoto.com

Celebrating the Sacrament

In the Sacrament of Reconciliation, we listen to the Word of God. The priest may read from the Scriptures or ask us to read. We hear God's Word about his love and forgiveness. The Word of God helps us to love God and to love one another.

© Bill Wittman/www.wpwittman.com

Activity

God's Word is a light for our path. The Sacrament of Reconciliation will help you follow God's Word. In the Bible pages below, **complete** the New Commandment Jesus gave us.

Love one another as

John 13:34

Living Our Faith

God always gives us the grace to do what he asks of us. In the Sacraments, we receive grace, the gift of God's own life in us. Grace enables us to live the way God wants us to. Grace also helps us to develop habits that make it easier for us to avoid sin and do the right thing. These good habits are called virtues.

With My Family

As a family, brainstorm ways to make the Scriptures a greater part of your family life. List your ideas. Choose one idea and carry it out this week.

Heart to Heart

The Commandment of Love

The Ten Commandments are rules God first gave to the Jewish people, but he meant them for everyone.

When Jesus came, he taught us to obey all of the Commandments and he summed them up with just one: love. If we love God and love others, we will keep all of the Commandments! We will love God and keep his name holy. We will keep Sunday holy and pray to God in church. We will love and listen to our parents. We will not steal from people or say mean things about them. Instead, we will always treat all people with love and kindness. Keeping the Commandments helps us show and share God's love.

To love is not always easy. But it is always the right thing to do. How will you love God and others today?

© iofoto/shutterstock.com

Activity

The Ten Commandments are God's rules. They are good rules, because they help us love God and one another. You may have other rules that you follow at home or at school. **Look** at the rules below. **Tell** why they are good rules. Then **write** a good rule of your own at the bottom.

- Raise your hand before you speak. This is a good rule because

  _____

  _____

- Do your homework. This is a good rule because

  _____

  _____

- Say your prayers every day. This is a good rule because

  _____

  _____

Write one more good rule to follow. **Explain** why it is a good rule.

- Rule: _____

This is a good rule because

  _____

  _____

With My Family

Take time to have a family meeting about family rules. Take turns naming a family rule. Together discuss the reasons for these good rules.

We Pray Together

We Pray to Follow God's Word

Loving God,

your Word in the Scriptures reminds us that you
    are always with us.

Help us to follow your Word in the
    Ten Commandments.

Help us to follow your Word of love that Jesus
    gave us.

Help us keep your Word in our minds, on our
    lips, and in our hearts.

Send your Holy Spirit to guide us in following
    your Word each day.

We ask this through Jesus Christ, your Son.

Amen.

© Jason Martin/istockphoto.com

30

I Confess

Return to the Lord

Leader: God says, "Be sorry and return to me with all your heart."

All: God says, "Be sorry and return to me with all your heart."

Reader 1: If we do not obey our parents, what should we do?

All: God says, "Be sorry and return to me with all your heart."

Reader 2: If we say or do something mean to another person, what should we do?

All: God says, "Be sorry and return to me with all your heart."

Reader 3: If we take something that belongs to another person, what should we do?

All: God says, "Be sorry and return to me with all your heart."

Reader 4: If we do not tell the truth, what should we do?

All: God says, "Be sorry and return to me with all your heart."

Based on Joel 2:12

What Does It Mean to Repent?

Prepare for the Lord!

Not long before Jesus began to teach and heal people, a man named John was preaching in the desert. He was telling people about the coming of the Lord.

"Prepare your life for the Lord!" he said. "Admit your sins. Turn away from them. And be baptized as a sign that you have changed."

This man was known as John the Baptist. People from all around Judea, the Jordan River, and Jerusalem came to hear him.

John the Baptist had a simple way of life. He lived in the desert. Many people listened to his teachings, and he baptized them in the Jordan River.

Then one day, Jesus came to John the Baptist through the crowds. Jesus also asked to be baptized.

John was surprised. "You are the Lord. Why are you coming to me to be baptized? I need to be baptized by you."

Jesus replied, "Do this to fulfill God's will."

So, John baptized Jesus in the Jordan River. When Jesus came up from the water, the heavens opened. The Spirit of God came upon Jesus like a dove.

Then a voice from the heavens said, "This is my beloved Son."

Based on Matthew 3:1–6,13–17

Activity

John the Baptist talked to people about preparing their lives for the Lord. **Draw** one way that you can prepare your life for the Lord by helping your family or other people.

With My Family

As a family, share and talk about the picture drawn in response to the activity on this page.

We Ask for God's Forgiveness

© John Cowie/iStockphoto.com

John the Baptist told people to admit their sins, turn away from them, and change their ways. To admit sins, turn away from them, and decide not to sin again is to repent. Repentance is an important part of asking God to forgive our sins. Like the word *contrition,* **repentance** means that we are sorry and that we will try not to sin again.

When we repent, we ask for God's forgiveness in the Sacrament of Reconciliation. First, we think about our sins. Next, we confess them, or say them out loud, to the priest. This part of the Sacrament is called our **confession.** It is not always easy to say our sins out loud. But when we do, we show that we understand that we have done wrong. Mortal sins must be confessed. The Church encourages us to confess our venial sins too. The Sacrament of Reconciliation is also known as the sacrament of confession.

Finally, to show that we will do better, we pray a prayer or do a good action that the priest tells us to do. This is called a **penance.** The Sacrament of Reconciliation is also called the Sacrament of Penance.

Repentance, confession, and penance are part of **conversion.** Conversion is turning our lives back to God. Turning back to God means turning away from sin. It means trying not to sin again. We turn back to God, knowing he loves us. God wants us to be happy with him and with one another, now and always.

© jabejon/iStockphoto.com

Activity

We want to turn back to God because we know he loves us. **Draw** a picture showing God's love for you. **Draw** some of his gifts to you: animals and plants, food and clothing, and your family, your parish, and your friends.

Our Conscience Guides Us

© Juan Estey/iStockphoto.com

To be sorry for our sins, we must know them. God has given each of us a conscience so that we will know the difference between right and wrong, good and evil. Our conscience also tells us when something we have done is a sin.

As we grow, our conscience must grow too. We help our conscience grow when we put God's Word into practice. We do this when we pray, when we follow the teachings of Jesus and of the Church, when we listen to our parents, and when we hear the Word of God proclaimed at Mass or read his Word in the Bible.

Before we receive the Sacrament of Reconciliation, we look closely at, or examine, our conscience. An **examination of conscience** is thinking about our actions and any sins we may have committed. We think about ways we failed to follow the Ten Commandments and about ways we could have followed Jesus better.

Celebrating the Sacrament

After the priest welcomes us and reads the Word of God to us, we confess our sins to the priest.

When we are sorry for our sins, we get a new start. We rise to new life with Jesus! Then the priest gives us our penance.

© Bill Wittman/www.wpwittman.com

Activity

Make an examination of conscience now. Then **find** the secret message to God in the puzzle by coloring the spaces with an x.

(Puzzle with hidden message: GOD I AM SORRY)

Faith Highlights

The priest will never ever tell anyone else our sins. This rule of the Church is called "the sacramental seal of confession."

 **With My Family**

Have a family discussion about experiences of conversion in each of your lives.

Heart to Heart

The Courage of the Holy Spirit

This is a big secret that is really not so secret, but here it is: Nobody likes to think about what they have done wrong. We do not like to think about the things we have done to hurt others, or the ways we could have helped someone but didn't. Thinking about what we have done wrong is sometimes hard to do. It takes a little bit of courage. To have courage means "to be brave" and "to be willing to do something that is hard."

The Sacrament of Reconciliation asks us to think about what we have done wrong and to tell our sins to a priest. That might seem hard. But the Holy Spirit gives us courage. This means that the Holy Spirit will help us think about what we have done wrong. And this hard part leads to the best part: God's love and forgiveness! We will be filled with his new life again!

© Bill Wittman/www.wpwittman.com

Activity

You have learned many new words in this chapter. Do you remember what each word means? **Write** the number of the word in the heart next to its meaning.

1. **repentance**
2. **confession**
3. **penance**
4. **conversion**
5. **examination of conscience**

♡ a prayer or good action to show we will do better

♡ thinking about our actions, any sins we have committed, and how we could have been better followers of Jesus

♡ telling our sins to the priest during the Sacrament of Reconciliation

♡ being truly sorry for our sins and trying not to sin again

♡ turning our lives back to God

With My Family

Brainstorm ways people in a family can show repentance to one another after arguments or hurts. Then try to make these a part of your family's practices.

We Pray Together

We Pray to God Our Father

Let us pray to God our Father in the words that Jesus gave us:

Our Father,
    who art in heaven,

hallowed be thy name;

thy kingdom come,

thy will be done

on earth as it is in heaven.

Give us this day our daily bread,

and forgive us our trespasses,

as we forgive those who trespass against us;

and lead us not into temptation,

but deliver us from evil.

Amen.

© Bill Wittman/www.wpwittman.com

I Am Sorry

We Pray an Act of Contrition

Side 1: My God,
I am sorry for my sins with all my heart.

Side 2: In choosing to do wrong
and failing to do good,
I have sinned against you
whom I should love above all things.

Side 1: I firmly intend with your help,
to do penance,
to sin no more,
and to avoid whatever leads me to sin.

Side 2: Our Savior Jesus Christ
suffered and died for us.

All: In his name, my God, have mercy.

(Rite of Penance)

© Bill Wittman/www.wpwittman.com

How Do We Show We Are Sorry?

Jesus Forgives the Sorrowful Sinner

Jesus once met a man named Simon, who was a Pharisee. The Pharisees were a community of Jewish people whose religious traditions were very important to them. They looked down on those who did not keep God's rules as perfectly as they did.

In the city where Simon lived, there was a woman whose sins were well known. She was the type of person who would be unwelcome at Simon's house. But one day this woman heard that Jesus was dining at Simon's house. So she went there to meet him.

The woman had a flask, or container, of ointment. She stood by Jesus, weeping, and bathed his feet with her tears. Then she wiped his feet with her hair, kissed them, and anointed them with the ointment.

Simon and the others at his table did not like what they saw. They wondered why Jesus did not turn away this sinful person!

But Jesus said, "She may have had many sins, but she has shown great love. Look at what she has done. She is full of sorrow and love."

Jesus said to the woman, "All of your sins are forgiven. Your faith has saved you. Go in peace."

Based on Luke 7:36–40, 47–50

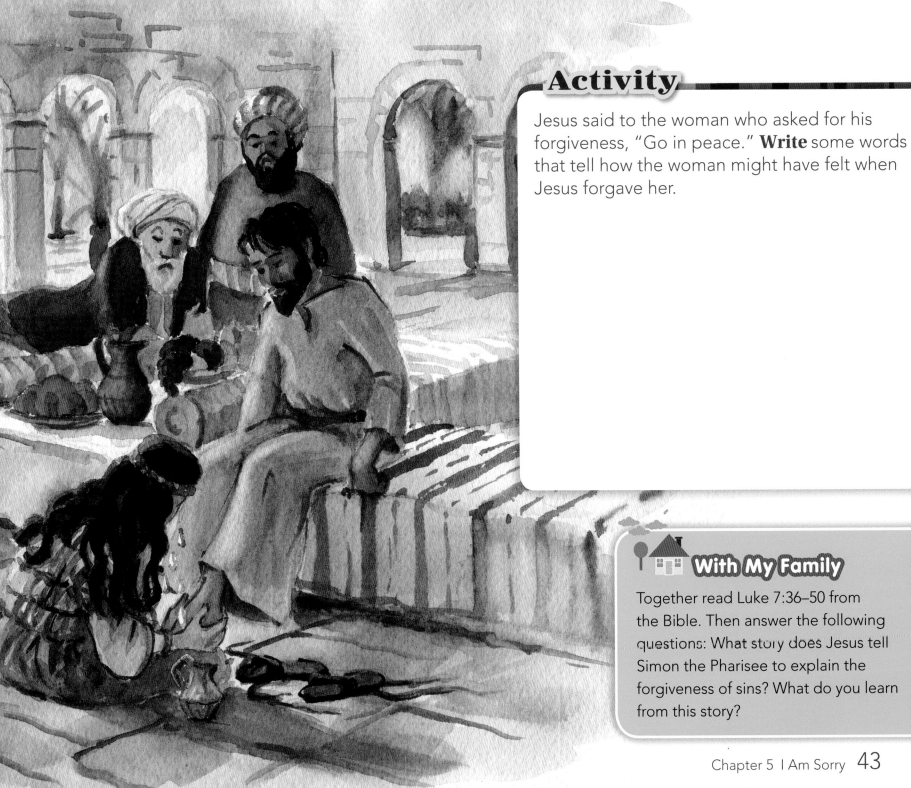

Activity

Jesus said to the woman who asked for his forgiveness, "Go in peace." **Write** some words that tell how the woman might have felt when Jesus forgave her.

With My Family

Together read Luke 7:36–50 from the Bible. Then answer the following questions: What story does Jesus tell Simon the Pharisee to explain the forgiveness of sins? What do you learn from this story?

We Are Sorry for Our Sins

The woman in the Scripture story came to Jesus looking for his mercy and forgiveness. She had so much love for Jesus and sorrow for her sins that she washed Jesus' feet with her tears. Jesus forgave all her sins, saying, "Your faith has saved you." The Scripture story teaches us that Jesus has mercy on sinners who have faith in him and sorrow for their sins.

In the Sacrament of Reconciliation, we come to Jesus looking for his mercy and forgiveness. Just like the woman in the Scripture story, each one of us is a **penitent.** A penitent is a person who has sorrow or contrition for his or her sins. As penitents, we confess our sins in the Sacrament of Reconciliation.

Of course we must be sorry for our sins. But our contrition must also include a resolve, or a firm decision, not to sin again.

© Anita Patterson-Peppers/istockphoto.com

44

The priest who celebrates this Sacrament with us has been given Jesus' power to forgive sins. Jesus granted this power to the first leaders of the Church, his Apostles. Jesus said to them, "Whose sins you forgive are forgiven them" (John 20:23). This power to act in the name of Jesus has been handed down to the leaders of the Church today, the Pope and the bishops. A priest receives the authority to forgive sins from his bishop.

Activity

We can talk to Jesus at any time and in any place. **Draw** yourself talking with Jesus. Then **ask** Jesus to help you come to him as a penitent in the Sacrament of Reconciliation.

_____

_____

_____

Celebrating the Sacrament

In the Sacrament of Reconciliation, we confess our sins as best we can. Then the priest offers us advice. He encourages us to do our very best to follow Jesus.

Then the priest gives us a penance to help us "start over." For our penance, the priest may ask us to pray or to help and serve others in some way.

Our penance shows that we are sorry. It helps repair the harm caused by our sins. It helps us make up for what we have done wrong. It helps us turn back to God our Father, and it helps us become better disciples of Jesus.

Two images on this page © Bill Wittman/www.wpwittman.com

After giving us a penance, the priest asks us to say a prayer expressing sorrow for our sins and our resolve to not sin again. This prayer is called an Act of Contrition, or a prayer of sorrow.

Activity

Use this secret code to uncover the name for a prayer we pray in the Sacrament of Reconciliation. **Find** the letter for each symbol and write it on the line.

Living Our Faith

After we pray the Act of Contrition or another prayer of sorrow, the next step in the Sacrament of Reconciliation is absolution, or the forgiveness of our sins. During absolution, the priest extends his hands (or right hand) over the penitent's head and asks God to forgive his or her sins. This is the sign of God's action in the Sacrament. You will learn more about absolution in the next chapter.

With My Family

Compose a family Act of Contrition. You might like to begin each line with a letter from your family's last name.

Heart to Heart

Being Sorry

Have you ever said, "That's not fair!"? Everyone likes things to be fair. We like fair rules that everyone must follow. We like things divided evenly. We think being fair is a good thing.

When the priest gives us a penance in the Sacrament of Reconciliation, it is one small way to make things even and fair again. If we hurt someone by our words and actions, it is only fair that we do something to make up for that hurt. Even though we cannot change what we did, we can show we are sorry. When God forgives us in the Sacrament of Reconciliation, we can do something— like the penance we are given—to show we are sorry, to show that we know we are responsible for our choices, and to show that we will try to do better next time.

© Image Source/Corbis

© sonya etchison/istockphoto.com

48

Activity

Read the story about Alex and Ramón. Then follow the directions given after the story.

Starting Over

Ramón sat in the church, praying silently. He had just celebrated the Sacrament of Reconciliation. He thought about the penance that the priest had given him. First he was to pray the Lord's Prayer. Then he was to do something kind for his brother Alex. Last week he had fought with Alex and called him a bad name. Now it was time to start over.

Ramón said the Lord's Prayer. Then he tried to think of something nice to do for Alex. Ramón had a dirt bike, and he knew his brother liked it. That was what started their fight in the first place! Alex had taken Ramón's bike—and not only that, he had brought it back all covered with mud.

Ramón also knew his brother liked to go fishing in the nearby pond.

Ramón decided he would ask his mother to walk to the pond with him and Alex. Ramón would take his dirt bike with him. On the way there and back, he would let Alex ride the dirt bike! He would keep this a secret to surprise his brother.

What do you think happened next? **Write** an ending for the story.

_____

_____

_____

Saint Spotlight

Mary, the Mother of God

The greatest saint of the Church is the Virgin Mary, the Mother of God. Mary was conceived and born without Original Sin. She remained free from sin her whole life. God chose her to be the mother of his Son, Jesus Christ. When we need forgiveness or help avoiding sin, we can ask Mary to pray for us and to bring our needs before God.

With My Family

Talk about ways you can start over during the times the people in your family do not get along or hurt one another.

We Pray Together

We Pray the Hail Mary

Hail Mary, full of grace,

the Lord is with thee.

Blessed art thou among women

and blessed is the fruit of thy

womb, Jesus.

Holy Mary, Mother of God,

pray for us sinners,

now and at the hour of

our death.

Amen.

© Jens Beuttenmueller/istockphoto.com

Pardon and Peace

We Sing a Song of Peace

"Peace Is Flowing Like a River"

Peace is flowing like a river,
Flowing out through you and me;
Flowing out into the desert,
Setting all the captives free.

Faith is flowing like a river,
Flowing out through you and me;
Flowing out into the desert,
Setting all the captives free.

Hope is flowing like a river,
Flowing out through you and me;
Flowing out into the desert,
Setting all the captives free.

Love is flowing like a river,
Flowing out through you and me;
Flowing out into the desert,
Setting all the captives free.

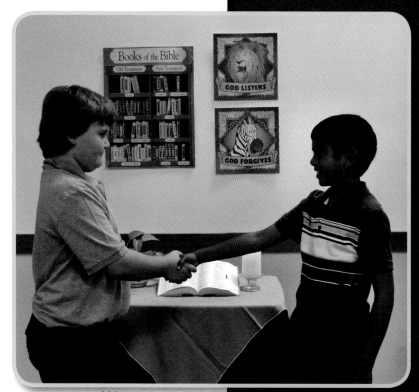

© Bill Wittman/www.wpwittman.com

Who Brings Us Peace?

Jesus Loves All People

Jesus traveled to many towns and cities, healing people and teaching them about God the Father's love and forgiveness.

One day, Jesus came to the town of Jericho. As he walked through the town, crowds of people followed him. One man had even climbed up into a tree to see him! He climbed the tree because he was not tall enough to see Jesus over the crowds.

The man, whose name was Zacchaeus, was very wealthy. He was a tax collector. In Jesus' time tax collectors were known to be dishonest people. They often became wealthy by stealing the tax money that they collected. But Zacchaeus wanted to follow Jesus.

When Jesus saw Zacchaeus in the tree, Jesus said, "Come down quickly, for today I must stay at your house."

Zacchaeus came down quickly and welcomed Jesus with joy.

The people grumbled, "Jesus has gone to stay at the house of a sinner."

But Zacchaeus told Jesus, "Lord, I will give half of my possessions to the poor. And I will pay back any money I have stolen—four times over!"

Jesus said to him, "Today salvation has come to this house."

Based on Luke 19:1–9

Write one thing that Zacchaeus did to show that he repented of his sins.

_____

_____

_____

What did Jesus say to Zacchaeus when he forgave him?

"Today ___ ___ ___ ___ ___ ___ ___ ___ ___
has come to this house."

With My Family

Talk together about times when family members lost something necessary or precious. Was it found again? At the end of this story from the Gospel of Luke, Jesus says to Zacchaeus, "For the Son of Man has come to seek and to save what was lost" (Luke 19:10). Talk about what Jesus means.

Jesus Brings Salvation

© Zvonimir Atletic/shutterstock.com

Our sins have a way of dragging us down. They may cause us to feel shame or guilt. They may nag at our conscience. They may cause people to turn away from us because we hurt them or they did not like what we did. And, as you have learned, sin hurts our relationship with God.

But Jesus says that he "has come to seek and to save what was lost" (Luke 19:10). Jesus seeks us out when we have sinned. He offers us new life. Jesus does not want our sins to drag us down anymore. He wants us to have **salvation.** He wants to forgive our sins. He wants us to enjoy a loving relationship with God, now and forever. He wants us to have loving relationships with everyone we know.

In the Sacrament of Penance and Reconciliation, Jesus gives us a chance to start again. Through the words and actions of the priest, God forgives our sins. This forgiveness is called **absolution.** When we receive absolution, it means that all of our sins are forgiven. No longer will our sins drag us down. We rise up again with Jesus.

When we receive absolution in the Sacrament of Reconciliation, we are given the gift of God's peace. After the priest absolves, or forgives, our sins, we can have peace of mind. The sins that have been forgiven should not nag at our conscience any longer. This peace is a sign of God's new life in us.

© Jani Bryson/istockphoto.com

Activity

"Absolution" means that our sins are forgiven, and we have God's peace. **Draw** a cross. Then **draw** yourself showing God that you are thankful and happy for his peace.

Celebrating the Sacrament

Absolution, the last step in the Sacrament of Reconciliation, takes place in the following way:

After the penitent prays an Act of Contrition, the priest, with his hands or hand over the head of the penitent, prays:

God, the Father of mercies,
through the death and resurrection of his Son
has reconciled the world to himself
and sent the Holy Spirit among us
for the forgiveness of sins;
through the ministry of the Church
may God give you pardon and peace,
and I absolve you from your sins
in the name of the Father, and of the Son,
and of the Holy Spirit.

Penitent: Amen.

(Rite of Penance)

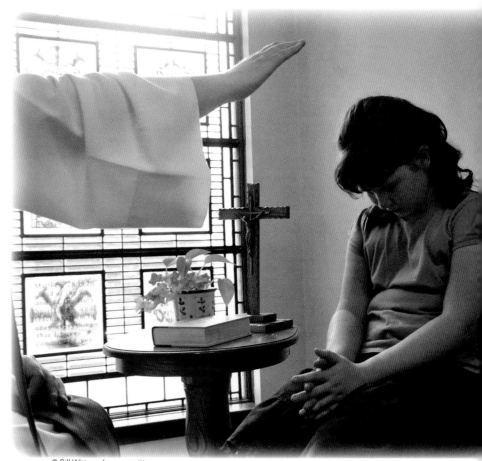

Through the priest's prayer of absolution, God gives us his pardon and peace. We are reconciled, or brought back together again, with God and with all his people, the Church. We are risen again with Jesus! We are ready to follow him again, even more closely.

Activity

Unscramble the words to find the message:

When the priest gives us absolution, God gives us his

_____
P N R O D A

and _____ .
P A C E E

We are _____
C C D E L E R I N O

with God and with the Church.

Faith Highlights

Every Sacrament has effects, or gifts, for us. These gifts truly change us. First of all, every Sacrament gives us grace, God's own life in us. As you have learned, one of the gifts of the Sacrament of Penance is peace. In the next chapter, we will learn about the many other gifts this Sacrament gives us.

With My Family

Peace is something that families need to strive for too. Brainstorm ways that your family can have more peace and harmony with one another.

Heart to Heart

Seeking Peace

A wise old saint named Benedict once said, "Seek peace and follow after it."

Sometimes we think peace will come without us doing anything about it. But that does not always happen. Sometimes we have to work for peace. Sometimes we have to make an effort to seek peace.

Zacchaeus made an effort to have peace in his heart. He climbed a tree to see Jesus! Then, after he heard Jesus speak, he promised to make up for all the wrong things he had done. If we want peace with our friends and our family, sometimes we have to work for it. We have to seek it. Say, for example, you had a disagreement with a friend. To make peace, you can go to your friend and talk things over. This will help your friendship be strong again, and you will have peace.

When we confess our sins in the Sacrament of Reconciliation, God forgives us. Our friendship with him becomes stronger and he gives us peace in our hearts.

Activity

In the billboard, **write** or **draw** about one way you can seek peace or work for peace.

Saint Spotlight

Saint Richard of Chichester (1197–1253)

Saint Richard of Chichester was a bishop in England. He helped his people follow God's rules and the teachings of Jesus. He especially loved and helped poor and needy people. He wrote a prayer asking to follow Jesus more closely. You might like to pray this prayer before or after celebrating the Sacrament of Reconciliation. You can find this prayer on the next page of this lesson or on page 93 at the back of this book.

With My Family

As a family, talk about the importance of "forgiving from the heart." (See Matthew 18:35.) God forgives us, but we must also forgive one another. Find out when your parish is celebrating its next communal celebration of the Sacrament of Reconciliation. If possible, plan for your family to attend, and for older family members to participate.

We Pray Together

We Pray to Jesus

O most merciful Redeemer, Friend, and Brother,

May I know you more clearly,

Love you more dearly,

And follow you more nearly,

Forever and ever. Amen.

(Saint Richard of Chichester)

His Mercy Endures Forever

We Praise God's Mercy

Leader: Give thanks to the Lord for he is good.

All: His mercy endures forever.

Reader 1: God made the heavens and the earth.

All: His mercy endures forever.

Reader 2: God made the sun, the moon, and the stars.

All: His mercy endures forever.

Reader 3: God gives food to all his creatures.

All: His mercy endures forever.

Leader: Give thanks to the God of heaven and earth.

All: His mercy endures forever.

Based on Psalm 136:1–9,25–26

How Can We Stay Close to Jesus?

Jesus Is the Good Shepherd

One day, tax collectors and sinners were gathered around Jesus, listening to him teach.

But the Pharisees and scribes complained, "This man welcomes sinners and eats with them."

When Jesus heard what they said, he told this story:

> A shepherd had one hundred sheep. One day, one of the sheep strayed from the rest of the fold and became lost. The shepherd left the other ninety-nine sheep to look for the lost one. When he found the lost sheep, he set it on his shoulders with great joy.
>
> He took the sheep home and brought it back into the fold. He called his friends and neighbors together. "Rejoice with me," he told them, "because I have found my lost sheep!"

After Jesus told the story about the sheep, he said, "In just the same way, there will be more joy in heaven over one sinner who repents than over ninety-nine righteous people who have no need of repentance."

Based on Luke 15:1–7

Activity

We read in the Scriptures that Jesus is our Good Shepherd, and we are his sheep (see John 10:11). If we are lost, Jesus will always come to find us. What other message did Jesus teach in the story about the shepherd? **Color** the letters with sheep in them to show a message from Jesus.

With My Family

Together write a family prayer to Jesus, the Good Shepherd. You might wish to read John 10:11–18 together before you begin. In this passage, Jesus explains that he gives his life for us, his sheep.

The Good Shepherd Loves His Sheep

The Scripture story teaches us that Jesus loves us, no matter what. When we sin, we are like the lost sheep in the story. No matter what we have done to stray from Jesus, Jesus seeks us out. When we come back to Jesus, he rejoices. He brings us back to his flock, the Church.

After we sin, we come back to Jesus by receiving the Sacrament of Penance and Reconciliation. This Sacrament reconciles us with God and the Church. When we are reconciled with God and the Church, we receive God's own life in us, God's grace. This is one of the effects, or gifts, of the Sacrament of Reconciliation.

Two images on this page © Bill Wittman/www.wpwittman.com

Another gift of this Sacrament is **peace**—with God, with ourselves, and with others. The Sacrament of Reconciliation also gives us a peaceful conscience, which you learned about in chapter 6.

Jesus is our Good Shepherd. He loves and comforts us like lost sheep that have been found.

© Kzenon/shutterstock.com

The shepherd in this picture has lost one of his sheep. **Help** the lost sheep find its way back to the shepherd!

The Good Shepherd Keeps His Sheep Close

What gifts does the Sacrament of Reconciliation give us?

© alekso94/shutterstock.com

- Our sins are forgiven.

- We are given God's own life, grace. We rise with Jesus to new life.

- We grow closer to God and to all God's people, the Church.

- We are given pardon and peace—with God, with ourselves, with others.

- We are given a peaceful conscience.

- We are given grace and strength to avoid sin and live as a Christian.

- We are able to repair some of the harm to our relationships caused by our sin.

- We are helped to stay in friendship with God in this life so that we will be happy with him forever in Heaven.

- We are saved, if we've confessed a mortal sin, from being separated from God forever after we die.

- We are more ready than ever to follow Jesus!

In all these ways, Jesus, the Son of God and our Good Shepherd, keeps us close to him and to God, our loving Father, now and forever.

Celebrating the Sacrament

After receiving absolution, we praise God for his mercy and thank him for his goodness. The priest leads us in praising God:

Priest: Give thanks to the Lord, for he is good.

Penitent: His mercy endures for ever.

(Rite of Penance)

In this wonderful Sacrament, the Good Shepherd has found us and brought us back to his flock. We rejoice and are glad!

© Godbehear/shutterstock.com

Activity

Complete this sentence. Then **draw** a picture to illustrate your sentence.

I feel peace when I . . .

_____ .

Living Our Faith

The Precepts of the Church, the special laws of the Church, require that we confess our sins in the Sacrament of Reconciliation at least once a year. However, the Church encourages us to receive this Sacrament as often as we need to.

With My Family

The Sacrament of Reconciliation has so many wonderful gifts for us! Use the list on page 66 to talk together about each of these gifts.

Heart to Heart

Found by the Good Shepherd

Have you ever been lost, even for a few minutes? Do you remember how afraid you were?

Jesus understands how it feels to be lost. He told the story of the lost sheep and the shepherd to remind us that if we sin and feel like we are lost, he will be our Shepherd. Jesus will find us and bring us back to him. He never stops loving us.

© Monkey Business Images/shutterstock.com

© Rob Marmion/shutterstock.com

Activity

Draw a picture of yourself in a place where you feel happy and safe.

We Pray Together

We Pray to Jesus the Good Shepherd

An Echo Prayer

Leader: Lord Jesus, you are the Good Shepherd.

All: Lord Jesus, you are the Good Shepherd.

Leader: You call us by name to follow you.

All: You call us by name to follow you.

Leader: You guide us along the right path.

All: You guide us along the right path.

Leader: If we turn away from you or get lost,

All: If we turn away from you or get lost,

Leader: we know you will find us and bring us home.

All: we know you will find us and bring us home.

Leader: Because you are always with us, we are not afraid.

All: Because you are always with us, we are not afraid.

Based on John 10:14, Psalm 23:1–4, Luke 15:1–4

© Justin McDonald/istockphoto.com

Go in Peace

Jesus Blesses Us

Leader: One day people were bringing children to Jesus so he could lay his hands on them and bless them. His disciples wanted to send the children away! But Jesus said,

Reader 1: Let the children come to me.

All: Alleluia!

Reader 2: Do not stop them.

All: Alleluia!

Reader 3: For the kingdom of God belongs to those with childlike trust.

All: Alleluia! Alleluia! Alleluia!

Based on Luke 18:15–16

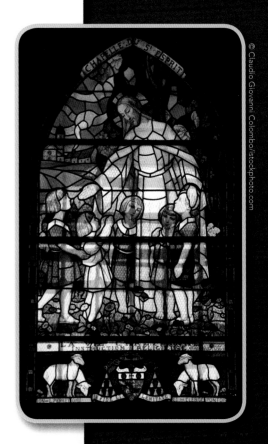

What Happens *after* the
Sacrament of Reconciliation?

Jesus Gives Us Peace

Jesus said to his disciples, "Those who love me will keep my word. They will be one with me and with my Father. They will live in my Father's love."

"Those who do not love me will not keep my word," Jesus explained. "My word is not my own. It is from the Father, who sent me."

Then Jesus told his disciples, "My Father will send the Holy Spirit to you in my name. The Holy Spirit will guide you and remind you of all that I have told you."

Then Jesus gave his disciples these words of encouragement: "Peace I leave with you; my peace I give to you. Do not let your hearts be troubled or afraid."

Based on John 14:23–27

72

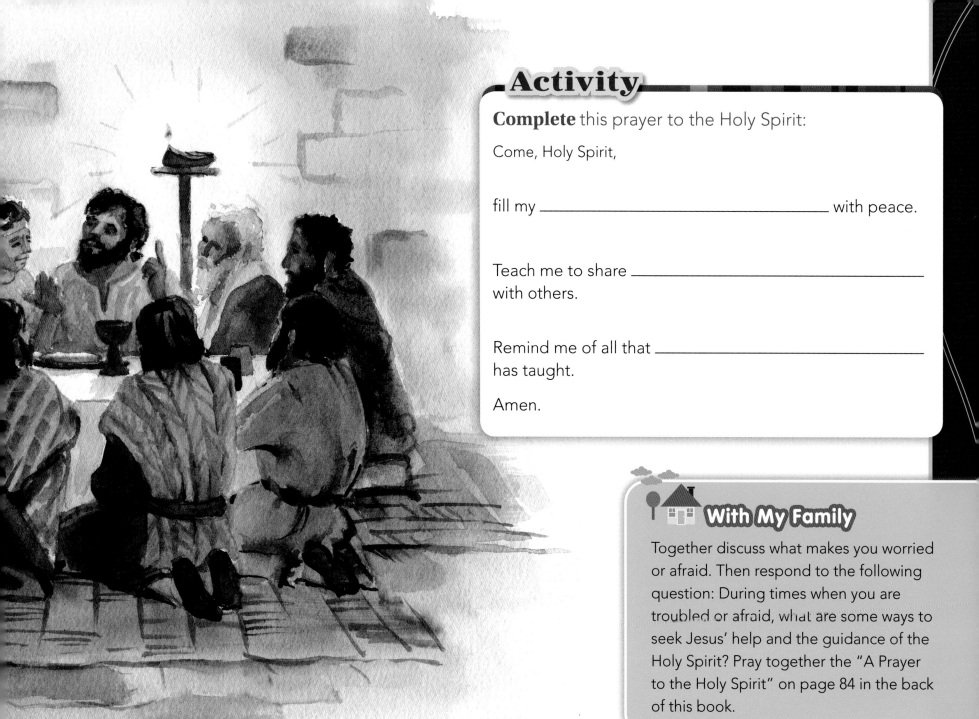

Activity

Complete this prayer to the Holy Spirit:

Come, Holy Spirit,

fill my _____ with peace.

Teach me to share _____ with others.

Remind me of all that _____ has taught.

Amen.

With My Family

Together discuss what makes you worried or afraid. Then respond to the following question: During times when you are troubled or afraid, what are some ways to seek Jesus' help and the guidance of the Holy Spirit? Pray together the "A Prayer to the Holy Spirit" on page 84 in the back of this book.

Jesus Keeps Calling Us to Conversion

Jesus keeps calling us to conversion. Jesus keeps calling us to turn away from sin and to turn toward God. We do not do this only once. We do this our whole lives!

The Sacrament of Reconciliation helps us live as disciples of Jesus. To be a disciple means to follow Jesus, to keep his teachings and Commandments. As disciples of Jesus, we try to follow him each and every day.

Jesus calls us to a life of goodness, a life without sin. This may sound difficult, but we do not do it all by ourselves. The Holy Spirit helps us. The Holy Spirit reminds us of all Jesus has taught us. The Holy Spirit guides us to do what is right.

Two images on this page © Bill Wittman/www.wpwittman.com

Celebrating the Sacrament

At the very end of the Sacrament of Penance and Reconciliation, the priest dismisses the penitent who has been reconciled. The priest says, "The Lord has freed you from your sins. Go in peace" *(Rite of Penance)*.

We are free of sin! We have new life in Jesus! **Alleluia!** (This means "Praise God!")

We must always remember to do our penance as soon as possible after celebrating the Sacrament of Penance and Reconciliation. We can also pray to Jesus, our Good Shepherd, in our own words, asking him to help us follow him more closely each day.

Activity

Draw a picture of yourself showing how will feel after you have received the Sacrament of Reconciliation. **Write** the word ALLELUIA! under your drawing.

_____

We Are Easter People

The most important day of the whole year for disciples of Jesus is Easter. Easter is the day Jesus rose from the dead. On Easter we sing over and over, "Alleluia, alleluia, alleluia." We are so happy that Jesus is risen and gives us new life, now and forever!

One of the greatest saints of the Church, Saint Augustine, wrote, "We are Easter people, and Alleluia is our song!" At Baptism, we became Easter people. We were given new life.

© Bill Wittman/www.wpwittman.com

© Lawrence Wee/shutterstock.com

In the Sacrament of Reconciliation, we rise with Jesus. Through this Sacrament and all the other Sacraments, we share God's life. We share new life every time we choose good over evil and right over wrong. Every time we do something good for someone, or say something kind, or are a friend to someone who is sad or lonely, we are sharing the new risen life of Jesus. We celebrate Easter once a year, but we can share the new life of Jesus with others every day. Every day we can say, "I am an Easter person. Alleluia!"

Activity

Imagine that you are meeting Jesus face-to-face. **Circle** one word you think he would say to you. **Draw** a symbol for this word.

Love   Hope   Joy   Peace

Faith Highlights

One of Jesus' teachings that can guide our lives is the Golden Rule: "Do to others whatever you would have them do to you" (Matthew 7:12). When we treat others the way we would like them to treat us, our actions are more kind and loving. Try to remember to follow the Golden Rule each day.

With My Family

Play "Name That Disciple" as a family. Take turns writing down each family member's strengths on a slip of paper. Put the slips of paper in a box or a bag labeled "Disciples of Jesus." Have each family member draw a slip and read it aloud as the others try to "name that disciple," the family member described on the slip.

Heart to Heart

Following Jesus

At Baptism, Jesus called us to follow him. But he keeps calling us each day. He sends the Holy Spirit to us to help us live a life of love. We do not do this all at once. We do it day by day, one step at a time. This path is not always easy to walk, but when we walk with Jesus, he brings joy to our hearts.

Conversion Road

Jesus calls us to be his disciples. How can you follow Jesus after receiving the Sacrament of Reconciliation? Write one way on each one of the eight stones. Some ways to follow Jesus might be: choosing right over wrong, listening to Mom and Dad, helping others.

**Saint Francis of Assisi
(1181–1226)**

Saint Francis of Assisi is a popular saint. He was born in Italy. As a boy, he grew up in a wealthy family. But when he was older, he gave everything he had to the poor. He also started the religious order called the Franciscans. They live a simple life of poverty and peace. Saint Francis's peace prayer is an important prayer. Our Pope Francis took his name from the name of this great saint.

 **With My Family**

Pray Saint Francis's peace prayer together. It can be found on page 93 at the back of this book.

We Pray Together

We Are Easter People!

Leader: Let us pray with the words of Saint Augustine, who said, "We are Easter people and Alleluia is our song!"

All: We are Easter people and Alleluia is our song!

Reader 1: When we love Jesus and keep his word,

All: We are Easter people and Alleluia is our song!

Reader 2: When we let Jesus' gift of peace help us when we are worried or afraid,

All: We are Easter people and Alleluia is our song!

Reader 3: When we comfort someone who is sad or lonely,

All: We are Easter people and Alleluia is our song!

Reader 4: When we ask for God's forgiveness in the Sacrament of Reconciliation,

All: We are Easter people and Alleluia is our song! Alleluia! Alleluia! Alleluia!

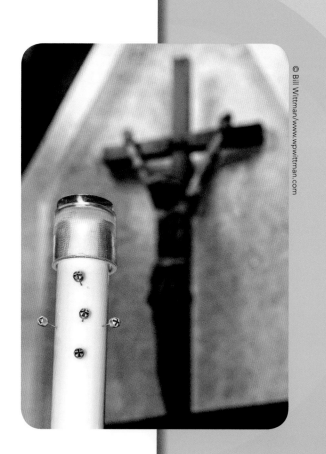

© Bill Wittman/www.wpwittman.com

Where We Celebrate Reconciliation

The Sacrament of Reconciliation

The Communal Celebration

1. We gather with our parish community. We join in singing a hymn. The priest greets us and leads us in praying together.

2. We listen to the Word of God. We may hear more than one reading, with a psalm response in between. We stand for the Gospel. Then we listen to a homily. The homily helps us understand what we heard in the Scriptures.

3. We make an examination of conscience. We think of things we have done that we are sorry for. We pray together to tell God we are sorry. Then we pray the Lord's Prayer together.

4. We wait to take our turn confessing our sins individually. While we wait, we can sing or pray. When it is my turn, I confess my sins. The priest gives me my penance and absolves me from my sins. My sins are forgiven! I make the Sign of the Cross with the priest.

5. When everyone has confessed individually, we pray and sing in thanksgiving to God. The priest or deacon blesses us. We go in peace.

6. I do my penance as soon as possible.

© The Crosiers/Gene Plaisted, OSC

The Individual Celebration

1. I take time to ask the Holy Spirit to help me remember what I have done or not done to follow God's rules. I think about the words of Jesus ("Love one another"), the Ten Commandments, and the Golden Rule (page 85). I examine my conscience.

2. The priest welcomes me. We make the Sign of the Cross together.

3. We read the Word of God. The priest may ask me to read.

4. I confess my sins to the priest. He may give me some words of advice or encouragement. Then he gives me my penance.

5. The priest invites me to pray an Act of Contrition. In my prayer, I tell God that I am sorry for what I have done wrong, and that I will try not to do these things again.

6. The priest extends his hands or right hand over me and gives me absolution in the name of Jesus. My sins are forgiven! I make the Sign of the Cross with the priest.

7. We give thanks to God, and then the priest sends me forth in peace. I do my penance as soon as possible. I quietly thank Jesus for giving me his new life of grace and a new start.

Receive the Sacrament of Reconciliation often. It will help you to follow Jesus. The Church wants us to receive this Sacrament at least once a year. Those who have committed a mortal sin must confess their sins and receive absolution before receiving Holy Communion.

© Tamara Bauer/istockphoto.com

An Examination of Conscience

Think about the words of Jesus: "Love one another as I have loved you."

Think about the Ten Commandments and the Golden Rule (page 85).

Ask the Holy Spirit to bring to your mind what you have done, or what you have not done, to follow God's rules. You may want to pray this prayer:

A Prayer to the Holy Spirit

Come, Holy Spirit, fill the hearts of your faithful

And kindle in them the fire of your love.

Send forth your Spirit and they shall be created.

And you shall renew the face of the earth.

© Juan Estey/iStockphoto.com

Ask Yourself

- Have I used God's name and the name of Jesus with respect?
- Have I honored God by saying my prayers?
- Have I done my best to pay attention at Mass and to pray and sing with my parish?
- Have I shown love to my parents and others who care for me by listening to them and always doing as they ask?
- Have I lied to my parents or my teachers?
- Have I been helpful to my brothers and sisters? Have I been mean to them?
- Have I treated others in a kind and friendly way? Or have I been mean to others?
- Have I played fairly?
- Did I call names or tell lies about someone?
- Did I share my things with others?
- Have I treated the belongings of others carefully? Have I taken what does not belong to me?

Catholic Prayers and Practices

The Golden Rule

"Do to others whatever you would have them do to you."

(Matthew 7:12)

The Ten Commandments	Way to Live the Commandments
1. I am the Lord your God, you shall not have other gods before me.	Make God the center of your life.
2. You shall not take the name of the Lord your God in vain.	Respect God's holy name.
3. Remember to keep holy the Lord's Day.	Participate in Mass on Sundays and Holy Days of Obligation. Set aside Sundays for prayer and rest.
4. Honor your father and your mother.	Love and obey your parents and those who are in charge of you.
5. You shall not kill.	Take care of living things. Respect life. Do not give in to anger or fighting.
6. You shall not commit adultery.	Respect marriage. Respect your body and the bodies of others.
7. You shall not steal.	Respect other people's property or belongings. Do not take what is not yours. Do not cheat.
8. You shall not bear false witness against your neighbor.	Tell the truth. Do not gossip or harm another's reputation.
9. You shall not covet your neighbor's wife.	Be respectful and pure in your thoughts and actions.
10. You shall not covet your neighbor's possessions.	Thank God for his blessings and share them with others. Do not be jealous, envious, or greedy for more things.

Based on Exodus 20:1–17

The Beatitudes

The Beatitudes	Way to Live the Beatitudes
Blessed are the poor in spirit, for theirs is the kingdom of heaven.	Remember that God is more important than anything else in your life.
Blessed are they who mourn, for they will be comforted.	Comfort those who are suffering, and when you suffer, remember that God will bring you comfort.
Blessed are the meek, for they will inherit the land.	Remember that winning isn't the goal of life. Be kind to others and put their needs ahead of your own.
Blessed are they who hunger and thirst for righteousness, for they will be satisfied.	Strive to do what is right and to be fair to others.
Blessed are the merciful, for they will be shown mercy.	Be a loving person.
Blessed are the clean of heart, for they will see God.	Develop habits that make it easier to avoid sin and to seek forgiveness when you sin.
Blessed are the peacemakers, for they will be called children of God.	Resolve disagreements with others peacefully.
Blessed are they who are persecuted for the sake of righteousness, for theirs is the kingdom of heaven.	Do the right thing even if others around you don't or even if you think someone will make fun of you.

Based on Matthew 5:3–10

The Precepts of the Church

1. Participate in Mass on Sundays and holy days of obligation. Keep these days holy. Avoid unnecessary work.

2. Confess your sins in the Sacrament of Penance and Reconciliation at least once each year.

3. Receive Holy Communion at least once a year, during the Easter Season.

4. Follow the rules of fasting and abstaining from meat on the special days of Ash Wednesday, Good Friday, and the Fridays of Lent.

5. Give what you can to help meet the needs of the Church.

The Holy Days of Obligation

Solemnity of Mary, Mother of God (January 1)

Ascension (40 days from Easter Sunday; may be celebrated on the last Thursday or Sunday before Pentecost)

Assumption of Mary (August 15)

All Saints' Day (November 1)

Immaculate Conception (December 8)

Christmas (December 25)

© Lawrence Wee/shutterstock.com

The Works of Mercy

Corporal Works of Mercy

1. Feed the hungry.

2. Give drink to the thirsty.

3. Clothe the naked.

4. Shelter the homeless.

5. Visit the sick.

6. Visit the imprisoned.

7. Bury the dead.

© Bill Wittman/www.wpwittman.com

Spiritual Works of Mercy

1. Counsel the doubtful.

2. Teach the ignorant.

3. Help the sinner.

4. Comfort the afflicted.

5. Forgive injuries.

6. Bear wrongs patiently.

7. Pray for the living and the dead.

© Jani Bryson/istockphoto.com

Sign of the Cross

In the name of the Father,
and of the Son,
and of the Holy Spirit.
Amen.

The Lord's Prayer

Our Father, who art in heaven,
hallowed be thy name.
Thy kingdom come;
thy will be done
on earth as it is in heaven.
Give us this day our daily bread;
and forgive us our trespasses
as we forgive those
who trespass against us;
and lead us not into temptation,
but deliver us from evil.
Amen.

© Bill Wittman/www.wpwittman.com

Glory Be to the Father

Glory be to the Father,
and to the Son,
and to the Holy Spirit.
As it was in the beginning,
is now,
and will be forever.
Amen.

Hail Mary

Hail Mary, full of grace,
the Lord is with thee.
Blessed art thou among women,
and blessed is the fruit of thy womb, Jesus.
Holy Mary, Mother of God,
pray for us sinners,
now and at the hour of our death.
Amen.

© Jens Beuttenmueller/istockphoto.com

The Apostles' Creed

I believe in God the Father almighty,
   creator of heaven and earth.
And in Jesus Christ, his only Son,
   our Lord, who was conceived by the Holy Spirit,
   born of the Virgin Mary, suffered
   under Pontius Pilate,
   was crucified, died, and was buried.
He descended into hell; the third day
   he rose again from the dead;
He ascended into heaven, and sits at
   the right hand of God the Father
   almighty; from thence he shall
   come to judge the living and the dead.
I believe in the Holy Spirit, the holy
   Catholic Church, the communion
   of saints, the forgiveness of sins, the
   resurrection of the body, and life
   everlasting. Amen.

© Zvonimir Atletic/shutterstock.com

Act of Contrition

My God,
I am sorry for my sins with all my heart.
In choosing to do wrong
and failing to do good,
I have sinned against you
whom I should love above all things.
I firmly intend, with your help,
to do penance,
to sin no more,
and to avoid whatever leads me to sin.
Our Savior Jesus Christ
suffered and died for us.
In his name, my God, have mercy.

(Rite of Penance)

Act of Hope

O Lord God, I hope by your grace for the pardon of all my sins, and after life here to gain eternal happiness because you have promised it who are infinitely powerful, faithful, kind, and merciful. In this hope I intend to live and die. Amen.

© John Cowie/iStockphoto.com

Prayer of Saint Francis of Assisi

(Peace Prayer of Saint Francis)

Lord, make me an instrument of your peace.
Where there is hatred, let me sow love;
where there is injury, pardon;
where there is doubt, faith;
where there is despair, hope;
where there is darkness, light;
where there is sadness, joy.

O Divine Master, grant that I may not so much seek to
   be consoled as to console;
to be understood as to understand;
to be loved as to love.

For it is in giving that we receive;
it is in pardoning that we are pardoned;
and it is in dying that we are born to eternal life.
Amen.

A Prayer to Jesus

by *Saint Richard of Chichester*

O most merciful Redeemer, Friend, and Brother,
May I know you more clearly,
Love you more dearly,
And follow you more nearly,
For ever and ever.
Amen.

© Bill Wittman/www.wpwittman.com

Glossary

A

absolution God's forgiveness of our sins through the words and actions of the priest

alleluia a word we pray that means "Praise God!"

C

confession telling our sins to the priest during the Sacrament of Reconciliation

contrition sorrow for our sins and a desire to avoid sin in the future

conversion turning our lives back to God

E

examination of conscience thinking about our actions, any sins we may have committed, and how we could have better kept the Ten Commandments and been better followers of Jesus

G

grace the free gift of God's own life in us which makes us his children

M

mercy love and forgiveness; we receive God's mercy in the Sacrament of Reconciliation

mortal sin a serious sin, committed on purpose, that completely breaks our loving relationship with God

O

Original Sin the first sin of humankind that has been passed on to us

P

peace an inner feeling of calm or quiet; peace is an effect, or gift, of the Sacrament of Reconciliation

penance a prayer or good action to show that we will do better

penitent a person who has sorrow for his or her sins and confesses them in the Sacrament of Reconciliation

R

repentance being truly sorry for our sins and trying not to sin again

S

Sacrament of Reconciliation the Sacrament in which God forgives our sins and brings us back together with him and with the Church

Sacraments seven holy signs that Jesus gave to the Church, which give us a share in God's life

salvation God's forgiveness of our sins so we can have a loving relationship with him, now and forever

sin something we say, do, or think that does not follow God's will. When we sin we offend God and hurt our relationship with him.

V

venial sin a less serious sin that weakens, but does not completely break, our loving relationship with God

Index

S

T

V

W

Z

I Have Completed First Reconciliation

May God Bless

_____ of _____,
(Name)   (Parish)

who received the Sacrament of Reconciliation for the first time

this _____ of _____, _____
        (date)   (month)   (year)

Signed

_____   _____

"I am an Easter person. Alleluia!"

Acknowledgments

The scriptural quotations in this book are from the *New American Bible with Revised New Testament and Revised Psalms.* Copyright © 1991, 1986, and 1970 by the Confraternity of Christian Doctrine, Washington, D.C. Used by the permission of the copyright owner. All Rights Reserved. No part of the *New American Bible* may be reproduced in any form without permission in writing from the copyright owner.

All other scriptural text throughout this book is freely adapted and is not to be interpreted or used as an official translation of the Bible.

The prayers, devotions, beliefs, and practices contained herein have been verified against authoritative sources.

The excerpts in this book marked *Rite of Penance* are from the English translation of *Rite of Penance* © 1974 by the International Commission on English in the Liturgy (ICEL), in The *Rites of the Catholic Church,* volume one, prepared by the ICEL, a Joint Commission of Catholic Bishops' Conferences (Collegeville, MN: The Liturgical Press, 1990). Copyright © 1990 by the Order of St. Benedict, Collegeville, MN. Used with permission of the ICEL.

"A Prayer to the Holy Spirit" on page 84 is from the English translation of "Come, Holy Spirit," in *A Book of Prayers,* © 1982, ICEL. Used with permission of the ICEL.

During this book's preparation, all citations, facts, figures, names, addresses, telephone numbers, Internet URLs, and other pieces of information cited within were verified for accuracy. The authors and Saint Mary's Press staff have made every attempt to reference current and valid sources, but we cannot guarantee the content of any source, and we are not responsible for any changes that may have occurred since our verification. If you find an error in, or have a question or concern about, any of the information or sources listed within, please contact Saint Mary's Press.

Notes

Notes

Notes

Notes